Food and Festivals

MEXICO

Linda Illsley

RSVP

RAINTREE
STECK-VAUGHN
PUBLISHERS
A Steck-Vaughn Company

Austin, Texas

Other titles:

The Caribbean • China • India
Mexico • West Africa

Cover photograph: A Mayan woman making *tortillas*

Title page: People taking part in the Corpus Christi Festival in the city of Veracruz

Contents page: A girl holding chilies

Published by Raintree Steck-Vaughn Publishers, an imprint of Steck-Vaughn Company

Printed in Italy. Bound in the United States.
1 2 3 4 5 6 7 8 9 0 03 02 01 00 99

Library of Congress Cataloging-in-Publication Data
Illsley, Linda.
Mexico / Linda Illsley.
    p.   cm.—(Food and festivals)
Includes bibliographical references and index.
Summary: Discusses some of the foods enjoyed in Mexico and describes special foods that are part of such specific celebrations as baptisms and weddings, Easter, the Day of the Dead, and Christmas. Includes recipes.
ISBN 0-8172-5553-2
1. Cookery, Mexican—Juvenile literature.
2. Food habits—Mexico—Juvenile literature.
3. Festivals—Mexico—Juvenile literature.
4. Mexico—Social life and customs—Juvenile literature.
[1. Cookery, Mexican. 2. Food habits—Mexico.
3. Mexico—Social life and customs]
I. Title. II. Series.
TX716.M4I4297 1999
641.5972—dc21   98-21844

CONTENTS

Mexico and Its Food

United States

N

NEW MEXICO

MEXICO

Mexico's place in the world

MEXICO

GULF OF MEXICO

PACIFIC OCEAN

YUCATÁN

Guadalajara

JALISCO

Mexico City

Pátzcuaro

Uruapan

Veracruz

MICHOACAN

Puebla

Taxco

GUERRERO

Oaxaca

BELIZE

CHIAPAS

GUATEMALA

HONDURAS

EL SALVADOR

| 0 | 400 km |
| 0 | 200 miles |

Corn

Corn is a cereal crop that grows all over Mexico. It is the most important crop in the country.

Wheat

Wheat is also a cereal. It is used to make bread and cake. Wheat is grown mainly in northern Mexico, where there is a good system of irrigation.

Chilies

Chilies have always been grown in Mexico. Most of the world's chilies still come from Mexico.

Beans

Beans are another important Mexican food. They contain lots of protein. Beans come in many different colors and sizes.

Fish

There are many types of fish available in Mexico. Red snapper is very popular.

Meat

Beef and pork are the most popular meats in Mexico. Cattle ranches are mostly in the north of the country.

5

Food and Farming

Mexico is a country just below the United States. It covers an area of almost 772,000 sq. mi. (2 million sq. km). Most of Mexico is covered by mountains, which makes it difficult to grow food. The climate varies from the hot and dry north to the humid heat of the south. The climate and landscape affect the types of food that are grown and the dishes that are prepared in each region.

A farmer and his child on their small farm in Chiapas state

There are many festivals in Mexico, and food plays a very important part in them. Mexican food is usually made from fresh ingredients.

Corn

Corn has been grown all over Mexico for hundreds of years. It is often planted in the traditional way, with zucchini and beans growing alongside. Corn is used to prepare hundreds of Mexican dishes, such as *tortillas*, which most Mexicans eat every day. Special dishes, such as *tamales*, are made by using ground corn.

▲ This painting shows the Tlaxcala Indians carrying and cooking corn in the early 1500s, about 500 years ago.

▼ A woman making *tortillas* in the traditional way

GIFT FROM THE GODS

The Amerindians, who first lived in Mexico, believed that corn was a gift from the gods. It was a sacred food, used in religious festivals. When Spanish explorers arrived in Mexico in 1492, the Amerindians replaced corn with wheat as their sacred food.

7

Wheat

Wheat is grown all over Mexico, but it grows mostly in the north. Large irrigation systems have been built there to provide the crops with water. Wheat is used to make bread and cake.

Festival bread

Bread is made from wheat. A special, traditional type of bread is made for the festival of the *Rosca de Reyes* (Day of the Three Wise Men), on January 6 each year. The bread has a tiny doll baked inside it. The person who gets the slice of bread containing the doll has to cook a meal for everyone else at a later date.

This bread has been specially prepared for the Day of the Dead (see page 22).

Chilies

More than 150 different types of chilies grow all over Mexico. They vary from the hottest chili, called *habanero*, to the mild chili, *güero*. Some chilies grow only in certain areas, such as the *chilhuacle*, which grows in Oaxaca. Chilies are used in many Mexican dishes. They add flavor and color.

These girls are holding a type of chili that is used in New Mexico.

FRESH OR DRIED CHILIES

Chilies are used in many festival dishes. *Chiles en nogada* is a dish made with fresh chilies, called *poblanos*, meat, nuts, raisins, and sour cream.

Dried chilies are called *pasilla*. They are used to make other foods, such as *enchiladas*. *Enchiladas* are *tortillas* covered with chili sauce, fried, and served with cream and cheese.

This market stand shows the many types of beans grown in Mexico.

Beans

Beans are the green pods of the bean plant, or the seeds inside the pods. Beans are very popular in Mexico because they grow easily. They are often planted next to corn crops. Beans are used in many Mexican recipes, and many special dishes are prepared with them.

THE DAY OF THE SACRED CROSS

Frijoles albañil is a bean dish cooked by builders on May 3 each year. This day is called the Day of the Sacred Cross, and builders cook this special dish in memory of the day when Jesus died on the cross.

TRADITIONAL RELIGIONS

There are 56 different peoples living in Mexico. Many follow the Roman Catholic religion, but they also keep some of their traditional religions and customs. For example, in some towns, live turkeys decorated with flower necklaces are carried to church as an offering. This tradition is believed to come from a pre-Columbian custom of sacrificing animals as offerings to the gods.

▲ At this festival in Oaxaca, a man carries a turkey decorated with flowers.

Meat

Meat is a favorite food in Mexico, so it is always served on special occasions and at festivals. In the north, there is lots of grazing land, so beef is more common. In the mountains and rain forests of the center and the south, it is easier to raise smaller animals, such as goats, pigs, chickens, and turkeys.

These chickens are ▶ being sold at a market.

Family Celebrations

About 90 percent of Mexicans are Roman Catholics. The Catholic religion was brought to Mexico by the Spanish in 1492.

Baptisms

Many Mexicans are baptized in church. There is a special baptism Mass (church service), to which all friends and relatives are invited. As they leave the church, the godparents of the baptized baby often throw coins into the air for the guests to catch. Children have fun running to try and catch the coins!

These girls are standing outside a church in Jalisco.

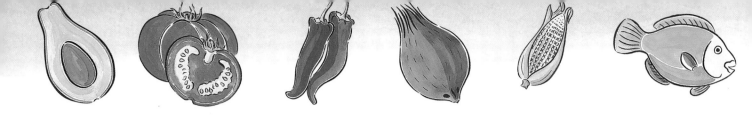

Party!

After the baptism Mass, there is a party at a rented hall or at the home of the baby's parents. A variety of food is served.

If the Mass is held in the morning, then a dish called *tamales* is often served. *Tamale* is a light, cornmeal dough, which is wrapped in corn husks and steamed. If the Mass takes place in the afternoon, people often eat a dish called *mole*. *Mole* has twenty-eight ingredients, including nuts, raisins, aniseed, chocolate, and three types of chilies. *Mole* is a sauce that is served with turkey or chicken and rice.

Tamales served with a bowl of *mole*

Birthdays

Many babies are named after Catholic saints. As they grow up, they celebrate the saint's birthday, as well as their own birthday. This means that Mexicans have two birthday parties a year!

A decorated cake and ice cream are often served at birthday parties, but dishes such as *pozole* and *tostadas* are also birthday favorites. *Pozole* is a soup or stew with meat, corn, and chilies. It is served with lemon, onion, oregano, and cabbage. *Tostadas* are fried corn *tortillas* topped with chicken and beans or pork and avocado. Cabbage, cream cheese, and *salsa* are often eaten with *tostadas*.

A typical "Sweet Fifteen" birthday party, traditionally a big day for girls in Mexico

Party game

A favorite game at Mexican children's parties is the traditional game of *piñata*. To make a *piñata*, a clay pot is filled with candy and fruit. It is covered with newspaper and decorated with colorful strips of paper to look like a figure or an animal. The *piñata* is hung up high.

Children line up for their turn to be blindfolded and given a stick, which they use to try and break the swinging *piñata*. When it is finally broken, everybody tries to grab the goodies that are inside!

This fruit stand in Mexico City has different types of *piñatas* hanging above it.

Weddings

▼ A recipe for making these Mexican wedding cookies is given on the opposite page.

Weddings can be the biggest event in many Mexicans' lives. More than 200 people are often invited to the church ceremony and to the party afterward.

At the party, after the wedding meal, the newlyweds cut a wedding cake covered with confectioners' sugar. There is usually a band for the guests to dance to, and the party may go on all night!

▼ *Mariachi* bands are very popular at Mexican weddings.

Wedding Cookies

EQUIPMENT

Greased baking tray
Chopping knife
Chopping board
Food processor
Large bowl
Wooden spoon
Sugar sifter

INGREDIENTS

1 cup shelled pecans
2 sticks unsalted butter, left
out to soften
$1/2$ cup sifted confectioners'
sugar
2 cups flour

1 Heat the oven to 350°. Roughly chop half the pecans. Put the other half in the food processor and grind them.

2 Put the butter, flour, and half the sugar into the bowl. Mix together to form a dough.

3 Add all the pecans and mix. Shape into small balls (about 24) and place them on the baking tray. Put the tray in the middle of the oven.

4 Bake for 10–15 minutes. Ask an adult to take the tray out of the oven. When the cookies are cool, sift confectioners' sugar on them.

Always be careful with hot ovens. Ask an adult to help you.

Easter

There are many religious festivals in Mexico throughout the year. Easter is one of the most important Christian festivals. On Good Friday, people remember Christ's dying on the cross, and on Easter Sunday, they celebrate his coming back to life. During Lent (the forty weekdays ending on the day before Easter Sunday), Catholics eat fish or lentils instead of meat. This is in memory of the time that Jesus spent in the desert without food.

Amerindian people acting out the events of Easter in a play

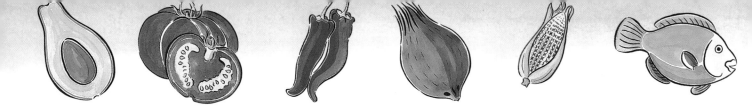

Easter processions

Some towns, such as Taxco and Iztapalapa (part of Mexico City), are famous for their Easter processions. The processions are always accompanied by bands of musicians.

People come from far away, either to watch or to take part in the processions. There are often street vendors selling many different types of food and drinks to the visitors.

A religious procession in Yucatán

Easter pottery

In some cities, such as Uruapan, there are special markets selling colorful, handmade pottery. It is traditional to buy a pot and give it to a friend. On the Saturday before Easter Sunday, you have to be careful if you walk through the streets, since it is also traditional to throw buckets of water over passersby!

▲ Mexican lentil soup with parsley, served with a *tortilla*. Follow the recipe opposite to make it yourself.

These women in Puebla are ▶ buying pots to give to their friends as traditional Easter gifts.

Lentil Soup

EQUIPMENT

Large saucepan
Wooden spoon

INGREDIENTS

2 Tablespoons oil
1/2 onion, finely chopped
1 clove garlic, chopped
4 bacon slices, cut into thin strips
3 tomatoes, chopped

6 1/2 oz. (185 g) lentils, washed
1 bay leaf
2 carrots, diced
1 qt. (1 l) water
Parsley
Salt and pepper, to taste

Put the oil, onion, garlic, and bacon in the saucepan and cook on medium heat until the onion changes color.

Add the tomatoes and cook for a few minutes, stirring constantly. Add the other ingredients except the parsley.

Bring the mixture to a boil over a high heat. Turn the heat down and simmer until the lentils are soft, stirring regularly.

Ask an adult to taste the soup. Add a little salt and pepper. Serve in soup bowls with some parsley in the middle. Eat with bread or *tortillas.*

Always be careful with hot liquids. Ask an adult to help you.

The Day of the Dead

The Day of the Dead is a Mexican festival based on a mixture of Catholic and Amerindian beliefs. Preparations for this festival take a lot of time. Special flowers are planted months ahead, and bread-baking ovens are built a week or so beforehand.

A girl in Michoacan decorating a grave for the Day of the Dead

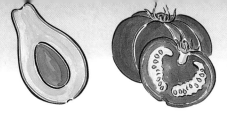

Tending the graves

On the last day of October, everyone goes to the cemetery to tend to the graves of dead friends or relatives. They decorate the graves with candles and flowers. At home, they build altars and place photographs of the dead people in the center.

▲ An altar in a family home in Guerrero. There is a photo of the dead relatives.

◄ People at a cemetery tending the graves of their ancestors on the Day of the Dead

Food offerings

Various types of food are placed on the altars or graves as an offering to the dead. Many Mexicans believe that the soul of a dead person returns on the Day of the Dead, shares a meal, spends some time with friends and relatives, and then returns to the world of the dead. Mexicans show their respect for death on this day.

◄ This is a decorated sugar skull for the Day of the Dead.

SUGAR SKULLS

On the Day of the Dead, it is traditional to buy sugar skulls to decorate the altar and the home. Sugar skulls are sold at special stands in markets. The foreheads of the skulls have a space where a name is written in sugar icing. People often buy skulls for the dead, as well as a skull for each living family member.

◄ *Salsa* is a sauce commonly served with every meal. Follow the recipe opposite to make the sauce called *salsa cruda*.

Salsa Cruda

EQUIPMENT

Chopping board   Spoon
Knife   Rubber gloves
Bowl

INGREDIENTS

1 small onion or
   6 green onions
   (scallions)
2 large, ripe tomatoes
Juice of 1 lime
Salt to taste
A few coriander leaves
2 *Serrano* chilies

Chop the onion or green onions. Chop the chilies, using rubber gloves.

Put the onion and chilies into the bowl. Add the lime juice and a pinch of salt.

Wash the tomatoes and the coriander and chop them into small pieces. Add them to the bowl and mix everything together with a spoon.

Leave the mixture for five minutes and then taste it to see if it needs more salt. Serve with *tacos* (filled *tortillas*), grilled meat, or *tortilla* chips.

**Always be careful when using knives. Ask an adult to help you.
Be careful handling chilies. The juice can burn your eyes.**

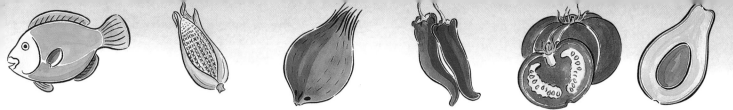

Christmas

Christmas is a Christian festival celebrating the birth of Christ. Christmas celebrations start early in Mexico, with traditional *posadas*, or nativity plays. These take place every night for the fourteen days before Christmas Day. Mexicans gather together with neighbors and friends to act out the story of Joseph and Mary's journey to Bethlehem. At the end of the play, candy and fruit are given out.

This is Guadalajara Cathedral, with a special nativity scene outside it for Christmas.

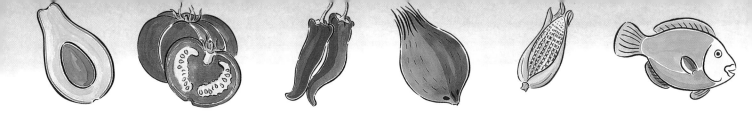

Christmas decorations on sale at a fair in Pátzcuaro

Christmas Eve

Mexicans have their big holiday dinner on Christmas Eve. The morning of Christmas Eve is very busy, because all the dishes for the big evening meal must be prepared. Stuffed turkey, *mole, tamales, buñuelos* (doughnuts), salads, cake, and other desserts are all traditional Christmas food.

There is a special Christmas Mass at church, where family and friends gather before the evening meal.

Dinner and dancing

This is a delicious Mexican Christmas drink. There is a recipe for it on the opposite page.

After Mass, many families go home to break a *piñata*. Some have two *piñatas*—one for the children, and a second one for the adults.

At the stroke of midnight, family and guests hug each other and wish each other a merry Christmas. They open presents while dinner is served. After dinner, music is played for everyone to dance to, often lasting until the next morning!

Christmas Drink

EQUIPMENT

Large saucepan
Bowl
Strainer

INGREDIENTS

5½ oz. (150 g) tamarinds, peeled

2 cups water

⅔ cup golden raisins

15 pitted prunes

5 cloves

10 fresh guavas, cut into small pieces (or 2 cans, drained and chopped)

1 cinnamon stick

Sugar to taste

Put the tamarinds and water into the saucepan. Bring to a boil and allow to simmer for 20 minutes.

Add more water, the cinnamon stick, cloves, and half the remaining fruit. Simmer for at least one hour.

Add some sugar. Ask an adult to taste the drink—it should be sweet, but not too sweet. Simmer for another five minutes until the sugar has dissolved.

Strain the liquid into a bowl. Allow the drink to cool slightly. Then pour into heat-proof glasses and decorate with the other half of the fruit.

Be careful with the hot pan. Ask an adult to help you pour the drink.

Glossary

Amerindians The native people of Mexico.

Baptism The Christian ceremony in which a person, often a baby, is welcomed into the Church.

Cereal Any grass that produces a grain that can be eaten, such as wheat, corn, or rice.

Godparent A family friend who agrees at a child's baptism to help the child learn about the Christian religion.

Grazing land Land where animals, such as cows, feed on grass.

Irrigation Bringing water to dry areas to help food crops to grow better.

***Mariachi* bands** Bands of strolling musicians who sing and play guitars, violins, and trumpets.

Mass A Roman Catholic service with a ceremony that celebrates Christ's death and his coming to life again.

Pre-Columbian The time before 1492, when Christopher Columbus arrived in the Americas.

Ranch A large area of land used for raising farm animals, usually cattle.

Roman Catholic A Christian religion headed by the Pope.

Sacred Having special religious meaning.

Soul The spirit of a person. The soul is believed to live on after a person has died.

Tortilla A thin pancake made of cornmeal and cooked on a hot, flat pan until it is dry.

Photograph and artwork acknowledgments
The publishers would like to thank the following for allowing their pictures to be used in this book:
Andes (Carlos Reyes-Manzo) 14; Chapel Studios (Zul Mukhida) 16 (top), 20 (top), 28; Getty Images (David Hiser) 20 (bottom); Hutchison (Liba Taylor) 8; Linda Illsley 10, 19; Image Bank (Guido Rossi) 5 (bottom left), (Jurgen Vogt) 12; James Davis Travel Photography (Eye Ubiquitous) 16 (bottom); Magnum *Cover photo*; Mexicolore (Sean Sprague) 18; Panos (Ron Giling) 6, (Liba Taylor) 13; South American Pictures (C. Lipson) 9, 11 (bottom), (Tony Morrison) 15, (Tony Morrison) 27; Trip (Ask Images) *Title page*, (C. Caffrey) 11 (top), (E. James) 22, (A. Deutsch) 23 (bottom), (C. Caffrey) 26; Mireuille Vautier 5 (top left), 5 (bottom right), 7 (top), 23 (top), 24 (top); Wayland Picture Library (Chapel Studios) 24 (bottom).

Fruit and vegetable artwork is by Tina Barber. The map artwork on page 4 is by Hardlines.
The step-by-step recipe artwork is by Judy Stevens.

Books to Read

Chambers, Catherine. *All Saints, All Souls, and Halloween* (A World of Holidays). Austin, TX: Raintree Steck-Vaughn, 1997.

Lewington, Anna. *Mexico* (Economically Developing Countries). Austin, TX: Raintree Steck-Vaughn, 1996.

Parker, Edward. *Mexico* (Country Insights). Austin, TX: Raintree Steck-Vaughn, 1997.

Silverthorne, Elizabeth. *Fiesta: Mexico's Great Celebrations*. Brookfield, CT: Millbrook Press, 1994.

Slim, Hugo. *A Feast of Festivals: Celebrating the Spiritual Season of the Year*. New York: HarperCollins, 1996.

Thompson, Jan. *Christian Festivals* (Celebrate). New York: Heinemann Library, 1997.

Index

Page numbers in **bold** mean there is a photograph on the page.